Written by   Wendy Loreen
Edited by   Linda Milliken
Design by   Wendy Loreen
Illustration by   Barb Lorseyedi & Priscilla Burris
Cover Illustration by   Priscilla Burris

© 1993 **Edupress** • P.O. Box 883 • Dana Point, CA 92629

ISBN 1-56472-013-6

TEACHER'S GUIDE

About the Games

All games are designed for hands-on, interactive learning. Construction is simple, with all game components made from recycled materials. Games are simple enough for most children to proceed independently. Younger children may need an adult or cross-age "helper."

Making the Games

Step-by-step directions and complete material lists are included to make game construction simple. Substitute materials where necessary. Enlist volunteers to help gather materials and make the games.

Playing the Games

Show children how to play each game by playing a practice game together. Become familiar with the skill objectives of each game. Help children learn and master the suggested game skills, paying attention to their individual needs.

Variations

Suggested game variations provide additional experience in other skill areas. Variations offer advanced skill practice while maintaining interest.

Additional Notes

Establish specific procedures for game selection and clean up. Game time will most likely be incorporated into lesson plans. However, allow students an opportunity to have a "free" game choice.

TABLE OF CONTENTS

Box Cars

Making the Game

Directions

1. Cut out the top and bottom of each box.

2. Paint the boxes primary colors.

3. Cut out two "hand holes" one inch from the top edge of each box, on two opposite sides.

4. Tape the "hand holes" with masking tape or colored plastic tape to protect from sharp edges.

Materials

- 1-24" x 24" x 24" (1- 60 cm x 60 cm x 60 cm) box (or close to this size) for each child

- Tempera paint in primary colors

- Masking tape or colored plastic tape

Playing the Game

How to Play

1. Have each student step into a "box car" and pick it up by the taped handles.

2. Line students up in random order.

3. Call out instructions such as, "Blue box cars move two steps left."

4. Repeat the instructions, varying the color of the box cars, number of steps taken, and direction.

Skill Objective

- Color recognition
- Directionality
- Listening/Transfer

Variations

- Add a second direction to each verbal instruction. "Blue box cars move 2 steps left and then 1 step back."

- Lay the boxes on their sides and have the children crawl through them on their knees.

- Create a tunnel maze and have the children slither through them like a "snake train".

PAINTER'S MATCH UP

Making the Game

Directions

1. Thoroughly clean and dry 8 empty coffee cans.

2. Be sure there are no sharp edges.

3. Cut construction paper to fit around each can. Cut a different color for each can.

4. Laminate the construction paper.

5. Wrap the construction paper around the can and tape to hold in place.

6. Paint each stirrer a color to match a can.

Materials

- 8 coffee cans
- 8 paint stirrers (available from paint stores)
- Construction paper
- Tape

Playing the Game

How to Play

1. Line the coffee cans in a row.
2. Match the color of the paint stirrer to a can.
3. Put the stirrer in its matching coffee can.

Skill Objective

• Hand-eye coordination
• Small motor
• Color identification

Variations

• Paste a number on the cans and put that many paint stirrers in them.
• Throw bean bags into the cans; have the children aim for all the different colors.

CLOTHESLINE CAPERS

Making the Game

Directions

1. Cut sheets of construction paper in half.

2. Paint different colored shapes on the construction paper such as circles, squares and triangles.

3. Hang the clothesline from two sturdy points in the classroom, low enough so that the children can easily reach it.

Materials

- Rope to be used as clothesline
- Clothespins
- Construction paper
- Paint or crayons

Playing the Game

How to Play

1. Lay all of the shapes on a table in front of children.

2. Call out a color and a shape and ask for volunteers to find the card matching that description then "hang it up to dry on the clothesline".

Skill Objective

- Color recognition
- Shape recognition
- Listening
- Small motor

Variations

- Laundry Letters: Paint letters on the construction paper and ask volunteers to spell their name on the clothesline.

- Have each child paint their favorite animal on a piece of construction paper. Hang up all of the "dogs" on the clothesline and count how many there are. How many cats? How many pigs!

RESPONSE POPS

Making the Game

Directions

1. Cut construction paper in 8" (20 cm) diameter circles—2 for each child in class.*

2. Glue the circles to the end of a popsicle stick, sandwiching the stick between them like a lollipop.

3. Have the children paint or color their pops with the words **YES** on one side and **NO** on the other.

   *2 white paper plates may be substituted for the construction paper.

Materials

- 1 popsicle stick or tongue depressor for each child in class

- Construction paper or white paper plates (2 for each child)

- Glue

- Paint or crayons

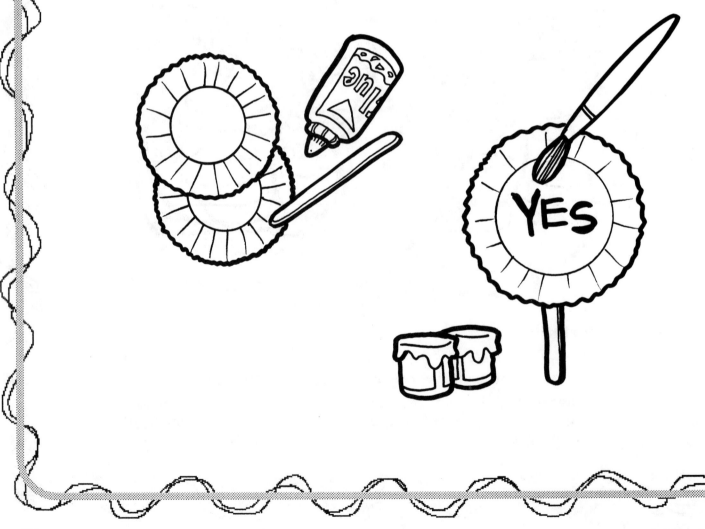

Playing the Game

How to Play

1. Give each child a "response pop".

2. Ask yes or no questions such as "Is the sun in the sky? Can a dog meow?"

3. Give the child with the most correct answers a special "response pop" lollipop.

Skill Objective

- Critical thinking
- Listening
- Vocabulary development

Variations

- Color Pops: "If your pop is red, hold it up."

- Body Pops: "Touch your pop to your knee. Touch your pop to your neighbor's back."

- Alpha Pops: "If you have the 'C', 'A', or 'T' pop, stand up and spell the word 'CAT'."

Sponge Match Up

Making the Game

Directions

1. Cut sponges into different shapes such as hearts, stars, circles and triangles.

2. Sponge paint one of each shape in different colors on a piece of construction paper to create the match-board.

3. Clean sponges and let dry as match-up game pieces.

Materials:

- Several sponges to cut shapes from
- Paint
- Construction paper

Playing the Game

How to Play

1. Set "sponge match-up" board in front of student.

2. Ask the student to match the sponge shapes to the painted corresponding shape on the board.

Skill Objective

• Visual matching
• Shape recognition
• Color recognition
• Small motor

Variations

• Cut the sponges in the same shape but in different sizes and paint match-up board.

• Have the children count the different types of shapes and colors.

• Have the children create their own match-up boards with pre-cut sponges. Ask the student with the most hearts to stand up. The most stars, etc.

Yarn Trails

Making the Game

Directions

1. Check for splinters on the wooden dowels. Sand if necessary.

2. Trim paper towel cores to 9" (22 cm).

3. Slide the dowels through the paper towel cores.

4. Wind the yarn around the paper towel cores.

Materials:

- 3 skeins of thick yarn in different colors

- 3 paper towel cardboard cores

- 3 wooden dowels, 1" (2.5 cm) diameter and 15" (38 cm) long

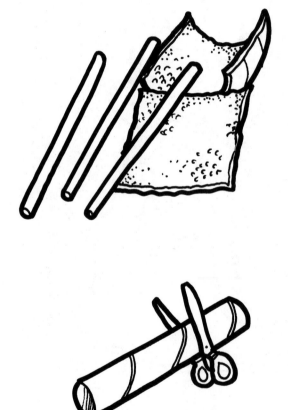

Playing the Game

How to Play

1. Make "yarn trails" by unraveling yarn from their spools onto the floor.

2. Loop the yarn around in circles and overlap the different colors.

3. Have the children stand anywhere on the "trails" and follow verbal instructions to "take five steps forward. Take two steps backwards".

4. Ask classroom monitors to "wind up" the trails when the activity is over.

Skill Objective

- Large motor
- Listening/Transfer
- Directionality

Variations

- Give verbal instructions to tiptoe on the trail; take baby steps; hop.
- Have the children jump from one color yarn to another.
- Place a "treasure" at the end of the trails and let children discover them.

PAINT PADS

Making the Game

Directions

1. Fill each bag with 3 tablespoons of finger paint. Vary the colors in the bags.

2. Reinforce all four sides with masking tape.

Materials:

- Finger paint
- Quart size zip-lock freezer strength bags
- Masking tape

Playing the Game

How to Play

1. Have children place a paint pad on the desk in front of them.

2. Call out different letters for the children to "paint" by tracing the letter with their finger on the paint pad.

3. Wipe pads clean with a swipe of the hand.

Skill Objective

• Alphabet recognition
• Small motor

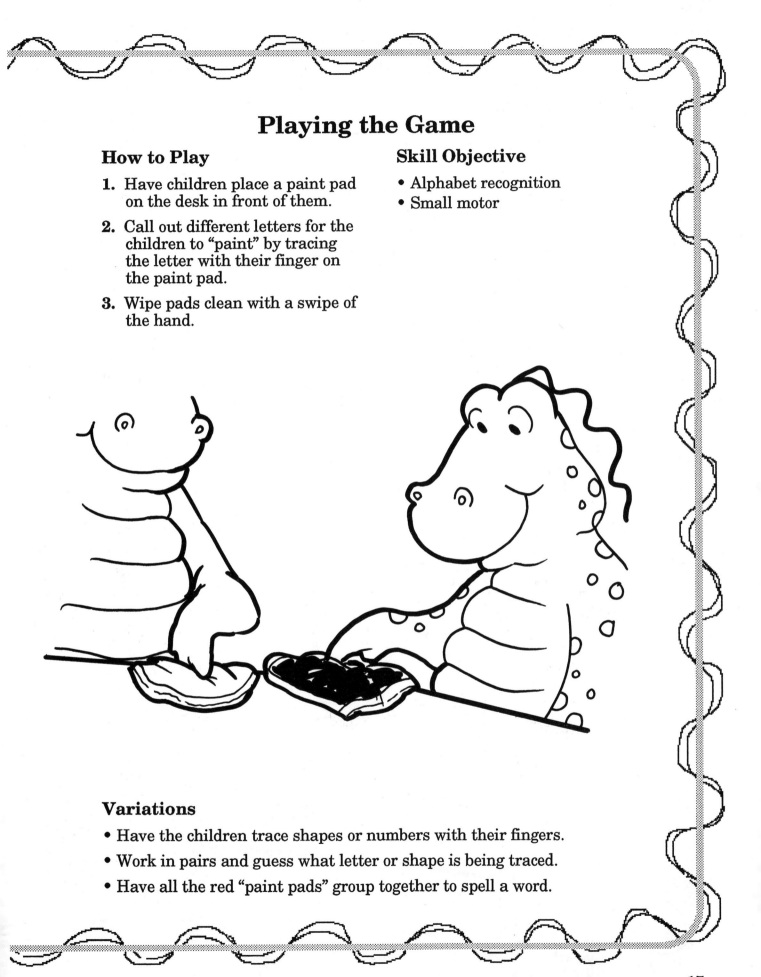

Variations

• Have the children trace shapes or numbers with their fingers.

• Work in pairs and guess what letter or shape is being traced.

• Have all the red "paint pads" group together to spell a word.

TENNIS BALL TUNNELS

Making the Game

Directions

1. Cut off the ends of the boxes to create "tunnels."

2. Paint the boxes different colors or cover with contact paper in different patterns.

3. Glue "tunnels" in a row in random order or by size to plywood or tagboard for easy cleanup.

Materials:

- Tennis balls (check with school tennis team or neighbors)
- Various size boxes
- Plywood or tagboard
- Paint or contact paper

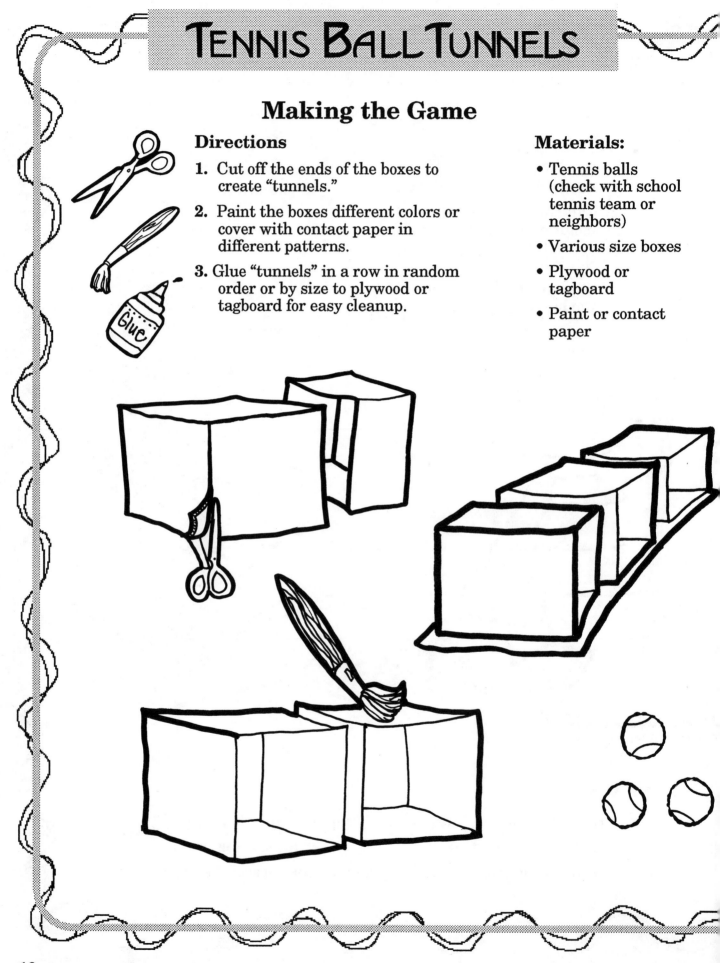

Playing the Game

How to Play

1. Set up the "tunnels" against a wall.

2. Place a masking tape line three feet in front of the tunnels.

3. Have students line up at the tape and roll the tennis balls into the tunnels.

4. Give verbal instructions to "roll into the largest box. Roll into the red box."

Skill Objective

- Large motor
- Color identification
- Listening/Transfer
- Size comparison

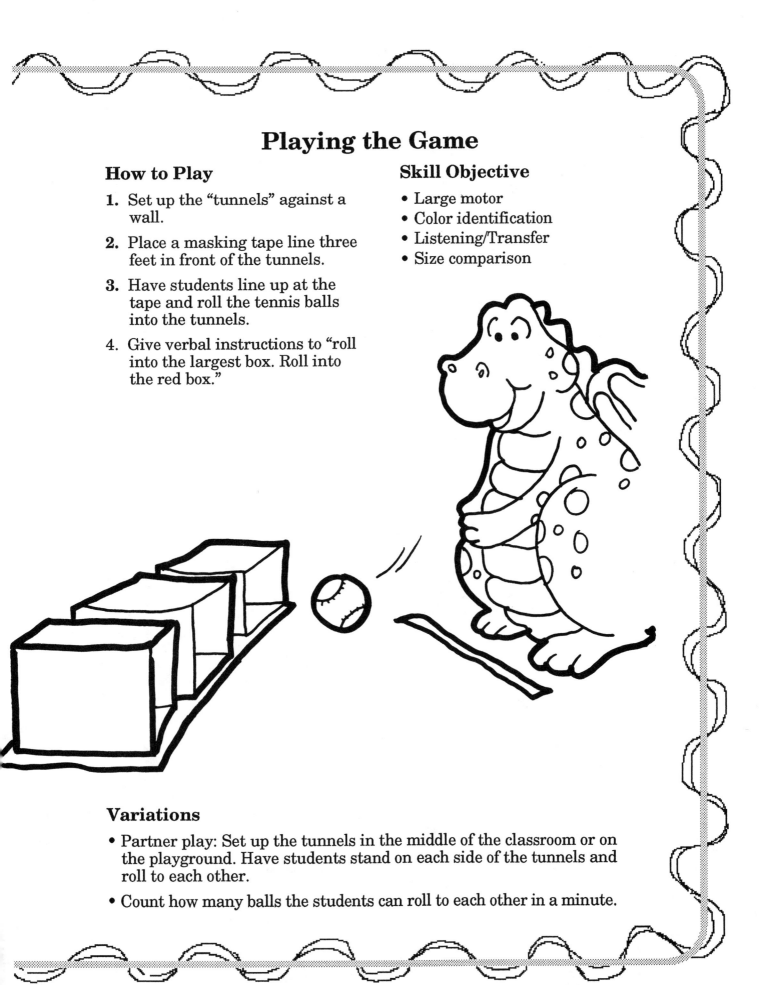

Variations

- Partner play: Set up the tunnels in the middle of the classroom or on the playground. Have students stand on each side of the tunnels and roll to each other.

- Count how many balls the students can roll to each other in a minute.

COUNTING TRAYS

Making the Game

Directions

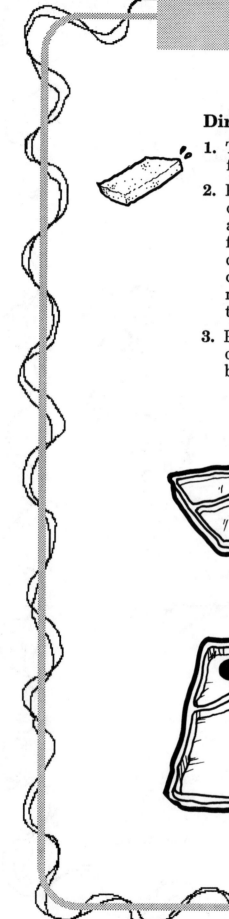

1. Thoroughly clean empty frozen food dinner trays.

2. Peel and stick color circles in each compartment of the tray. For example, put one red circle in the first compartment, two blue circles in the next, three green circles in the next, etc., using as many trays as needed to count to ten.

3. Place 55 (or more) buttons, beans or other type of marker in a zip top bag.

Materials:

- 3 or more TV dinner trays for a total of 10 compartments

- 55 peel and stick color circles

- 55 (or more) buttons, beans or other type of marker to fit on top of each circle

- Zip top bag to store markers.

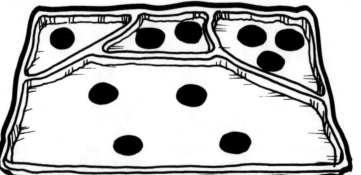

Playing the Game

How to Play

1. Set the counting trays and bag full of place markers on desk in front of children.

2. Have the children count to 10 aloud by placing a marker on each circle in all of the compartments.

3. As each marker is placed the children should count the number of circles in each compartment, such as : 1; 1, 2; 1, 2, 3; etc.

Skill Objective

- Counting
- Color recognition
- Hand-eye coordination

Variations

- Ask the children to place markers only on the yellow circles. Count how many there are. Place markers only on the red circles. Count how many there are.

- Use other shapes such as squares and triangles along with circles in the frozen food trays. Ask the children to place markers on all of the "blue squares" and count them.

Can Do Cans

Making the Game

Directions

1. Wash and dry empty cans.

2. Make sure there are no sharp edges where lid was removed.

3. Decorate the cans by applying contact paper or colored paper taped around the can.

Materials

- 4 or 5 different size cans that will stack inside each other

- Contact paper or colored paper to wrap around cans

- Tape

Playing the Game

How to Play

1. Set the cans on a table in random order.

2. Ask the student to line up the cans left to right from smallest to largest.

3. Now ask the student to stack the cans inside each other.

Skill Objective

- Small motor
- Size discrimination
- Left to right tracking

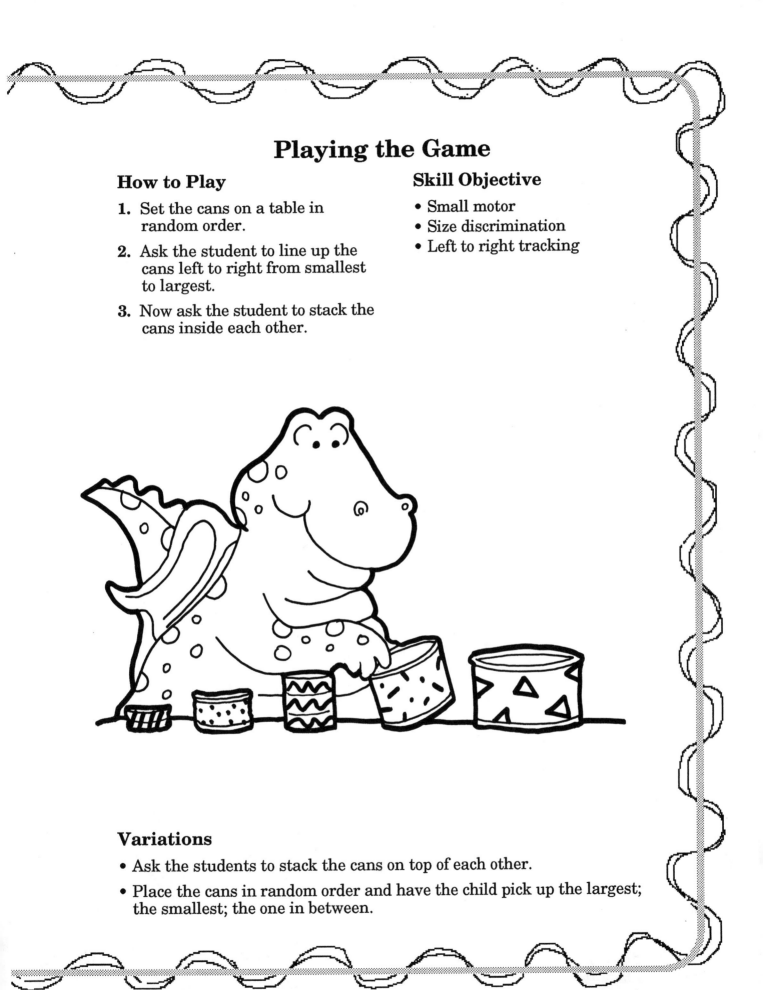

Variations

- Ask the students to stack the cans on top of each other.

- Place the cans in random order and have the child pick up the largest; the smallest; the one in between.

GARDENER'S GAME

Making the Game

Directions

1. Clean out the inside of the flower pak.

2. Fill each of the 6 compartments half full with clay or play dough.

3. Cut out 12 flowers in the shape of daisies. Glue a round yellow circle in the center. Make two of each colored flower.

4. Paint the popsicle or craft sticks green.

5. Glue the daisies to the green popsicle or craft stick "stems".

Materials

- 1 empty flower pak with 6 compartments

- Enough clay or play dough to fill the 6 compartments of the flower pak half way to the top

- 12 popsicle or craft sticks

- Green tempera paint

- 7 different colored sheets of construction paper

Playing the Game

How to Play

1. Separate the flowers into two matching sets.

2. Plant one set in the flower pak container by sticking the stems into the clay or play dough.

3. Place the other set on the table in front of the student. Mix them up.

4. Ask the student to pick a flower from the desk and match it to a flower in the pak. "Plant" it in the same compartment and watch as the flowers grow and fill up the pak.

Skill Objective

- Visual discrimination
- Small motor
- Color recognition

Variations

- Add difficulty to the game by increasing the number of flowers that the children have to choose from on the table. Vary the centers of the flowers also, and have the children make a perfect match.

- Add other shapes and colors of flowers to the set such as tulips, roses, or pansies.

- Create additional flower paks to increase the number of matches possible.

- Create a vegetable garden pak.

PICTURE THIS

Making the Game

Directions

1. Take close up pictures of different items in your classroom; the clock, pet mouse, cupboard handles, etc.

2. If an instant camera is not available, develop film into color prints. If possible have a "double" set of prints made for game variation.

3. Laminate the prints for durability.

4. Decorate a box to hold your classroom pictures.

Materials

- Instant or other type of camera

- Enough color print film so each child can have at least one picture

- Shoe box or other type to hold pictures

Playing the Game

How to Play

1. Hand each student a picture face down. Don't peek!

2. Ask students to look at the picture, and find the item in the classroom and stand by it.

3. When all of the students have found their items, collect the pictures, mix them up, and start again.

Skill Objective

- Visual discrimination
- Spatial awareness
- Object identification

Variations

- Pass out a picture to each student in the class. Ask each child to stand up and describe their picture without saying what it is. "It's round with numbers on it"...can the rest of the class guess the answer?..."The clock!"

- Lay the pictures on a table and ask students, one by one, to pick a picture whose object has a certain texture or color. Ask all the "red" pictures to stand in one area of the classroom. Ask all the "furry" pictures to stand together.

- If double prints are available, hand out one set of pictures to the children and lay the other set on a table face up. One by one have the children find their matching picture.

Making the Game

Directions

1. Glue the two wrapping paper rolls to the outside long edges of the poster board or tag board.

2. Have children personalize their own "log roll jumper" by decorating the poster board or tag board with crayons.

Materials

For One
Log Roll Jumper:

• 2 cardboard wrapping paper rolls

• One piece of poster board or tag board the length of wrapping paper rolls (about 30"-75 cm) and 16" (40 cm) wide

• Glue

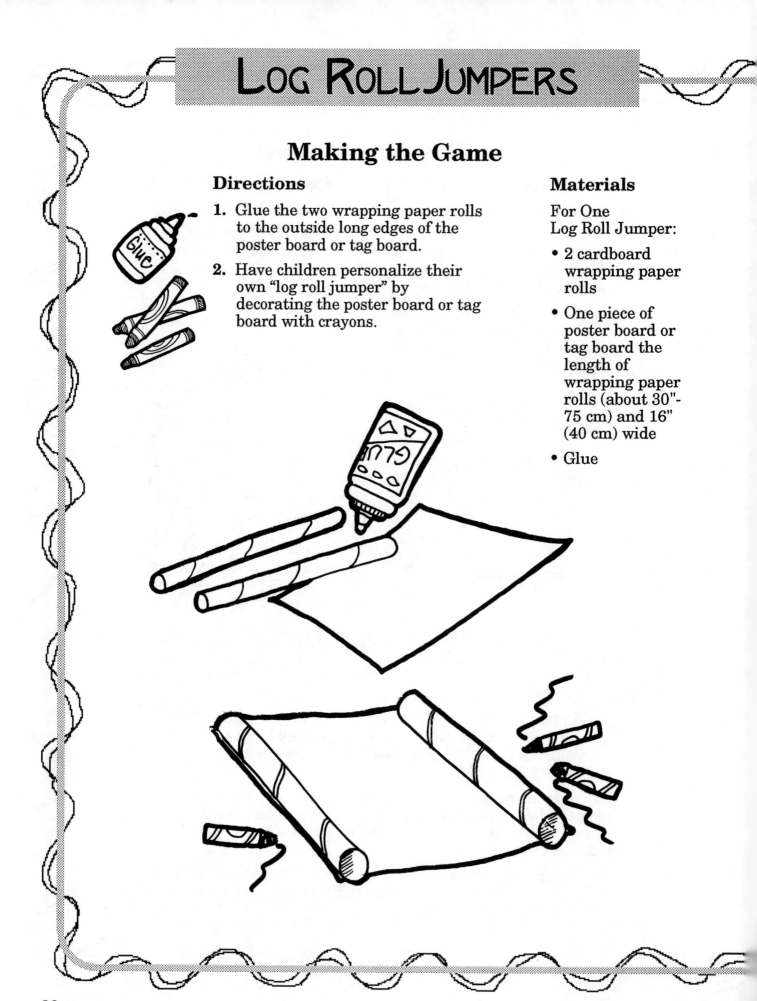

Playing the Game

How to Play

1. Each child should place a "log roll jumper" in front of them on the floor.

2. To start, have the students stand in between the "logs".

3. Call out instructions to "jump with both legs outside the logs, then both legs in; hop over each log with one foot, etc."

Skill Objective

- Large motor
- Laterality
- Listening/Transfer
- Locomotor skills
- Spacial awareness

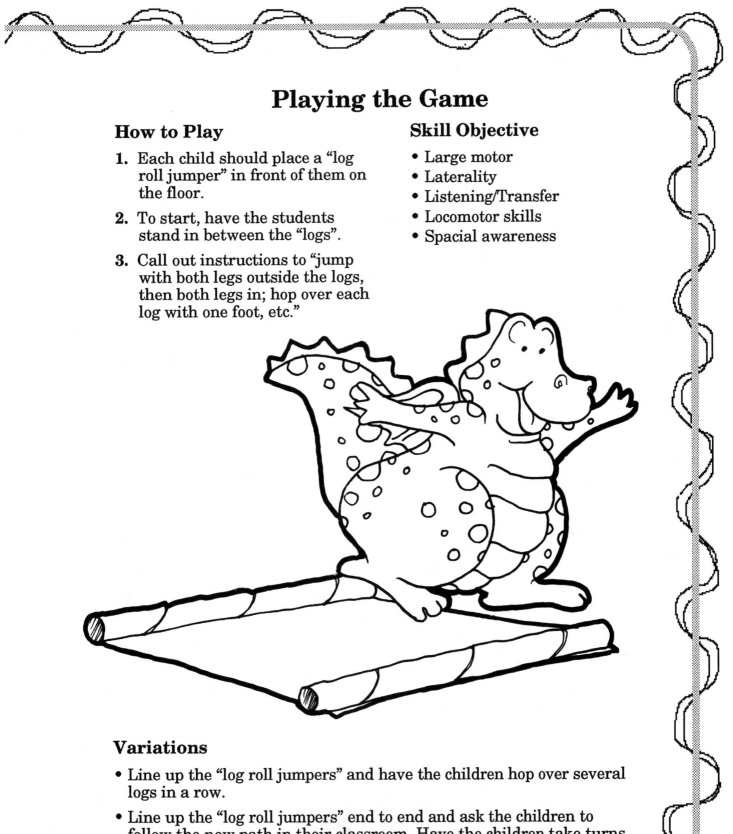

Variations

- Line up the "log roll jumpers" and have the children hop over several logs in a row.

- Line up the "log roll jumpers" end to end and ask the children to follow the new path in their classroom. Have the children take turns taking the last "log roll jumper" and placing it in front of the first one in a different direction. See where this path takes you!

BOX TOP TRACKERS

Making the Game

Directions

1. Draw zigzag, curved, and squiggly lines on the box top with pencil .

2. Cut out the different "tracks" so that the width of each is the same as a craft stick.

3. Decorate the box tops if desired.

Materials

- Sturdy box tops 1-2 inches (2.5 cm - 5 cm) in height

- 2-3 craft sticks for each "box top tracker"

- pencil

- scissors or blade knife

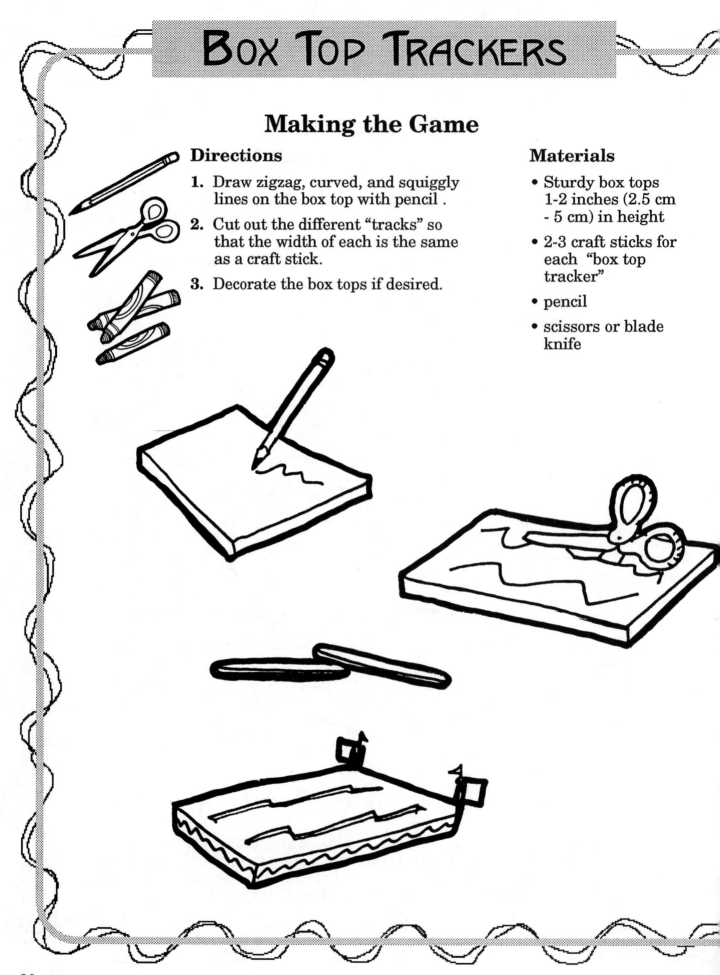

© Edupres

Playing the Game

How to Play

1. Place the box tops on the table with the top up so tracks are raised off the table.

2. Ask the students to take a craft stick and trace each track.

3. Call out directions for the student to "trace the zig zag track forward and backward".

Skill Objective

• Small motor
• Hand-eye coordination
• Visual tracking

Variations

• For more advanced students, turn the boxes over and place a marble inside the box. Roll the marble down one of the tracks by tilting the box forward.

Making the Game

Directions

1. Find a magazine picture of an animal or an image related to a theme currently being studied.

2. Line 4 small boxes in two rows of two, making sure that the combined top surface area of the boxes is not bigger than your picture.

3. Glue the picture to the top of all the boxes at once, as they are positioned next to one another.

4. Slice apart the boxes with your razor knife. Glue down any loose edges.

Materials

- 4 small boxes the same size
- Full page magazine picture
- Glue or spray glue
- Razor knife

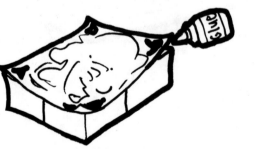

Playing the Game

How to Play

1. Place the "picture puzzler" on a table face up.

2. Ask children individually or cooperatively to recreate the picture.

3. For more advanced students, place several picture puzzlers mixed up on a table, and ask students to recreate the pictures.

Skill Objective

- Small motor
- Sequential development

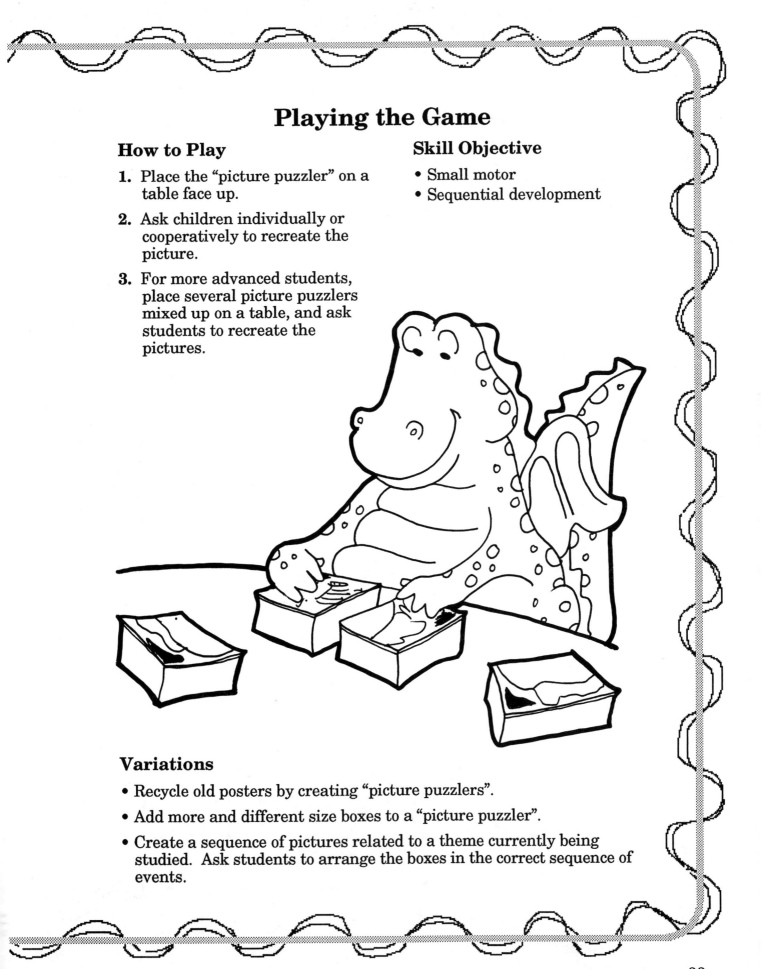

Variations

- Recycle old posters by creating "picture puzzlers".

- Add more and different size boxes to a "picture puzzler".

- Create a sequence of pictures related to a theme currently being studied. Ask students to arrange the boxes in the correct sequence of events.

TREASURE QUEST

Making the Game

Directions

1. Cut out a square 4" x 4" (10 cm x 10 cm) from the middle of the lid.

2. Cover the cut edges with plastic tape or contact paper.

3. Decorate the box and lid with paint or contact paper to look like a treasure chest.

4. Fill the box with sand about 3/4 full.

5. Add everyday classroom items to the box that have different textures and shapes such as a key, chalkboard eraser, pencil, etc.

Materials

- 1-12" x 12" x 12" (30 cm x 30 cm x 30 cm) box (or close to this size) with a lid.

- Tempera paint or contact paper

- Utility knife

- Masking or colored plastic tape

- Enough sand to fill the box 3/4 full

- Small everyday classroom items to put in the box as treasures. One for each student participating

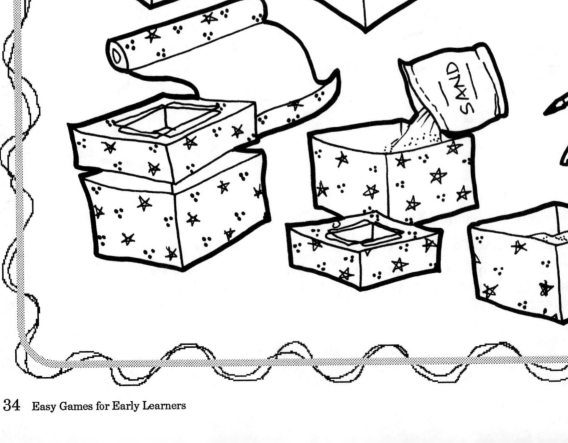

Playing the Game

How to Play

1. Pass around the treasure chest to each child participating.

2. Have each child reach into the treasure chest filled with sand.

3. Before revealing their treasure ask the child to guess what it is by touch alone.

Skill Objective

• Shape recognition
• Tactile identification
• Critical thinking

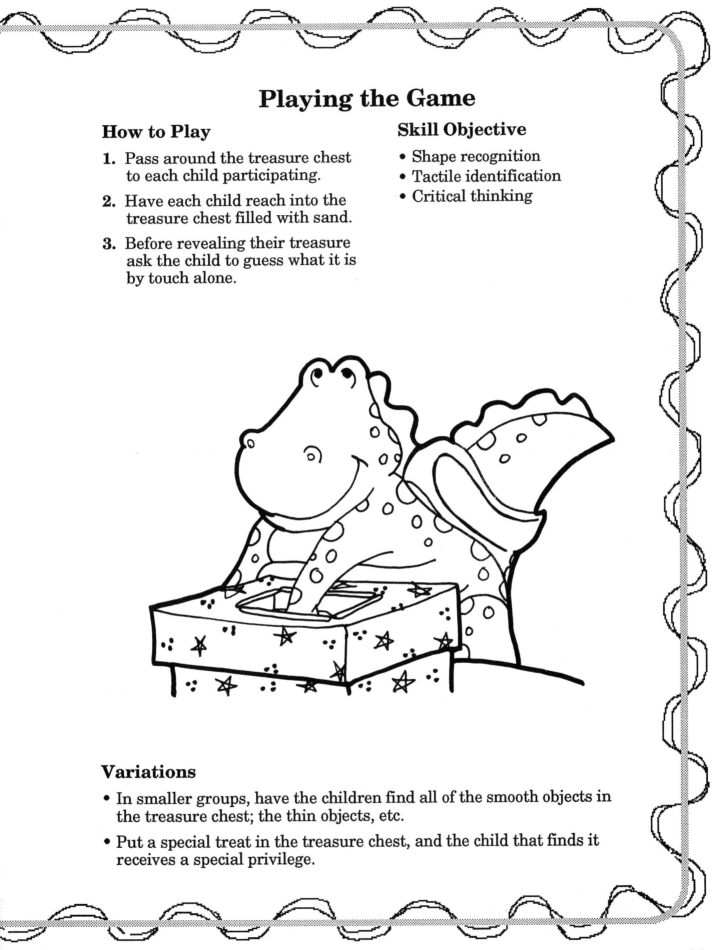

Variations

• In smaller groups, have the children find all of the smooth objects in the treasure chest; the thin objects, etc.

• Put a special treat in the treasure chest, and the child that finds it receives a special privilege.

CATEGORY BUFFET

Making the Game

Directions

1. Thoroughly clean the polystyrene meat trays.

2. Find pictures in magazines representing six different categories such as animals, transportation, food, etc. Find seven pictures for each category.

3. Cut out the pictures and mount them on construction paper.

4. For added durability laminate the pictures after mounting and cut out according to their shape.

5. Glue one picture from each category to a meat tray.

Materials

- 6 polystyrene meat trays from the grocery store
- Magazines
- Construction paper
- Glue

Playing the Game

How to Play

1. Place the six category trays on a table in front of the student.

2. Scatter the magazine pictures next to the trays.

3. Have the student place each magazine picture one by one in the appropriate category tray.

Skill Objective

- Categorizing
- Object recognition
- Critical thinking

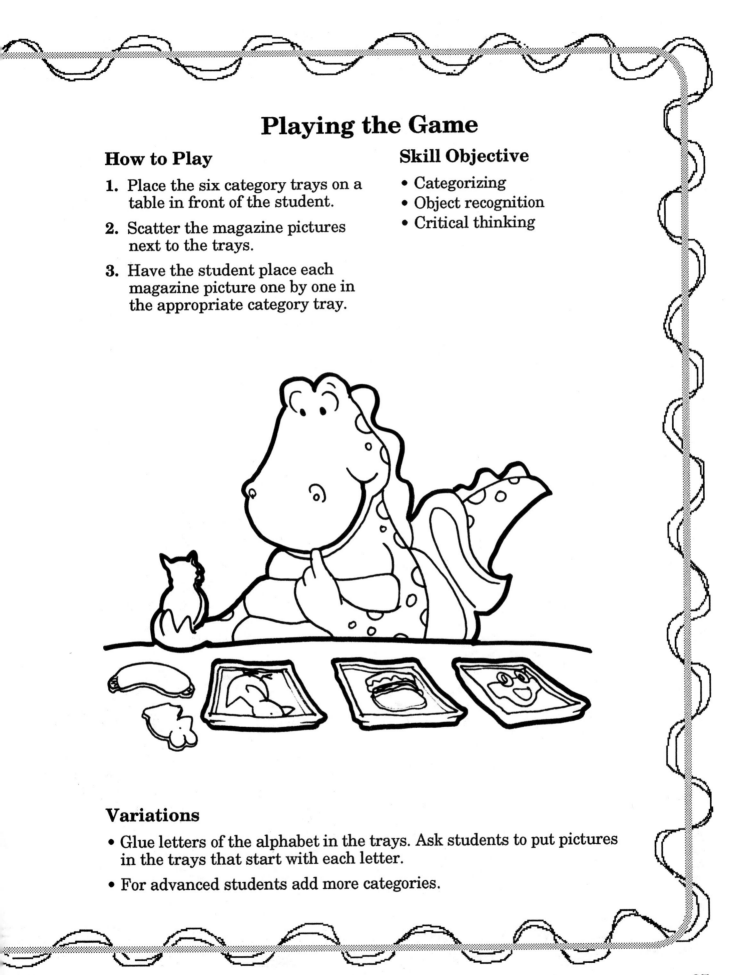

Variations

- Glue letters of the alphabet in the trays. Ask students to put pictures in the trays that start with each letter.

- For advanced students add more categories.

UTENSIL RELAY

Making the Game

Directions

1. On a long table set up the items in the materials list. Keep them in the same order as indicated, top to bottom, in the list.

Materials

- Egg beater
- Bowl of water
- Plate
- Salt shaker and pepper mill
- Spatula
- Sponge
- Tongs
- Pot scrubber
- Empty bowl

Playing the Game

How to Play

1. See how fast each child can get through the relay line.

2. Each child has to:

    *   beat the water
    *   shake salt and grind pepper onto the plate
    *   turn the sponge with the spatula
    *   pick up the pot scrubber with the tongs and put it in the empty bowl

3. Time each child as they "cook" through the relay.

Skill Objective

*   Small motor
*   Hand-eye coordination
*   Listening/Transfer

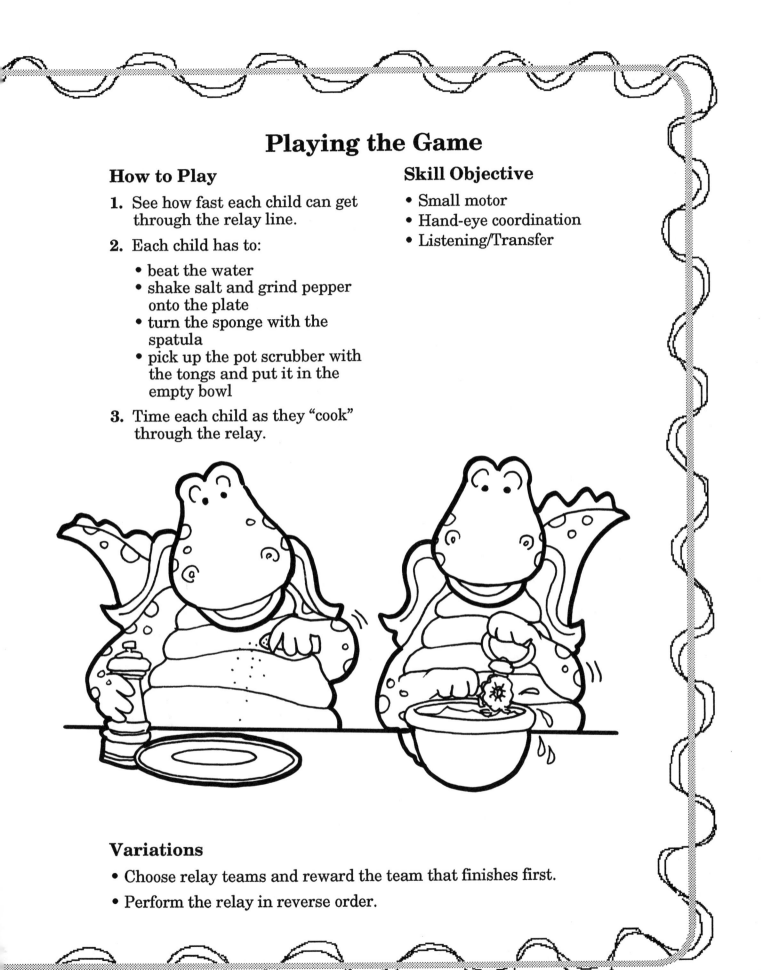

Variations

*   Choose relay teams and reward the team that finishes first.

*   Perform the relay in reverse order.

Making the Game

Directions

1. Cut off the top of an egg carton.
2. Cut the bottom in half along the length.
3. Cut out a piece of fabric that will cover one half of the egg carton.

Materials

- 1 egg carton
- Scissors
- 2 each of 6 items that will fit inside the egg cups (marbles, crayons, paper clips, etc.)
- A piece of fabric 9" x 14" (22 cm x 35 cm)

Playing the Game

How to Play

1. Place a different item in each of the six egg cups.

2. Give the child the six matching items and the empty half of the egg carton.

3. Show the first group of items in the egg cups to the child, then cover them with the cloth.

4. Have the child try to place the items in the empty cups in the same order.

5. Remove the cloth to see how well the child remembered.

Skill Objective

- Observation development
- Memory development
- Sequencing

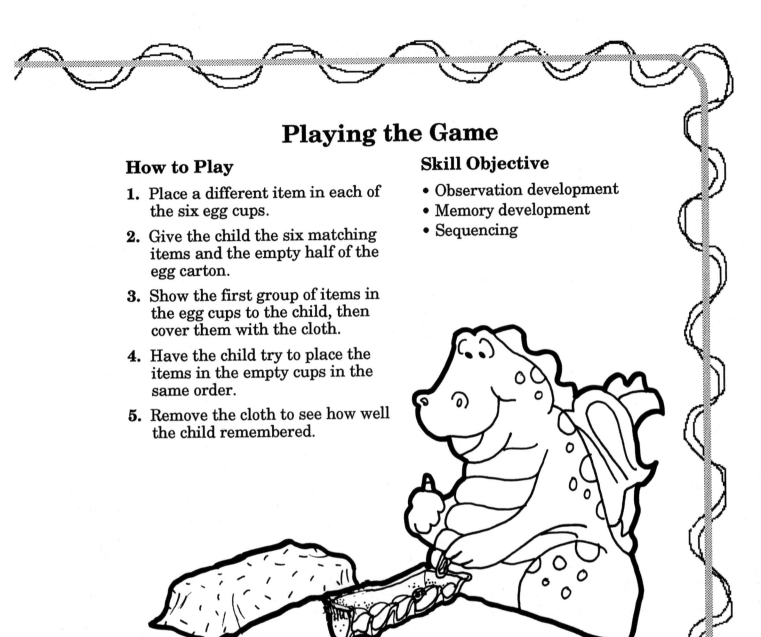

Variations

- For less advanced students, divide the egg carton into sets of three cups for memory match-ups.

- Have children play with partners and count how many items they can remember.

- For color recognition, put colored circles in the egg cups.

- For letter recognition, write the alphabet on small cards that will fit in the egg cups. Add letters to the game as children learn them.

TUBULAR TOWERS

Making the Game

Directions

1. Cut the cardboard tubes to four or five different lengths.

2. Cut the wooden dowels to match the different tube lengths. Sand, if necessary, to eliminate any rough edges.

3. Glue the ends of the tubes to the wood base so they are lined up next to each other from smallest to largest. Glue the sides of the tubes to each other to make it sturdier.

4. Decorate the tubes and base board. Leave the dowels plain.

Materials

- 4 or 5 lengths of cardboard tubes such as toilet paper rolls, paper towel rolls, wrapping paper rolls, etc.

- Light wooden dowels that will fit inside

- Scissors or utility knife.

- Glue

- A piece of wood 20" x 6" x 1" (50 cm x 15 cm x 2.5 cm)

Playing the Game

How to Play

1. Set the "tubular towers" on a table in front of the student.

2. Ask the student to choose one of the dowels and slide it into its matching tube.

3. If the student picks the wrong tube, turn over the towers and start again.

Skill Objective

• Small motor
• Size discrimination

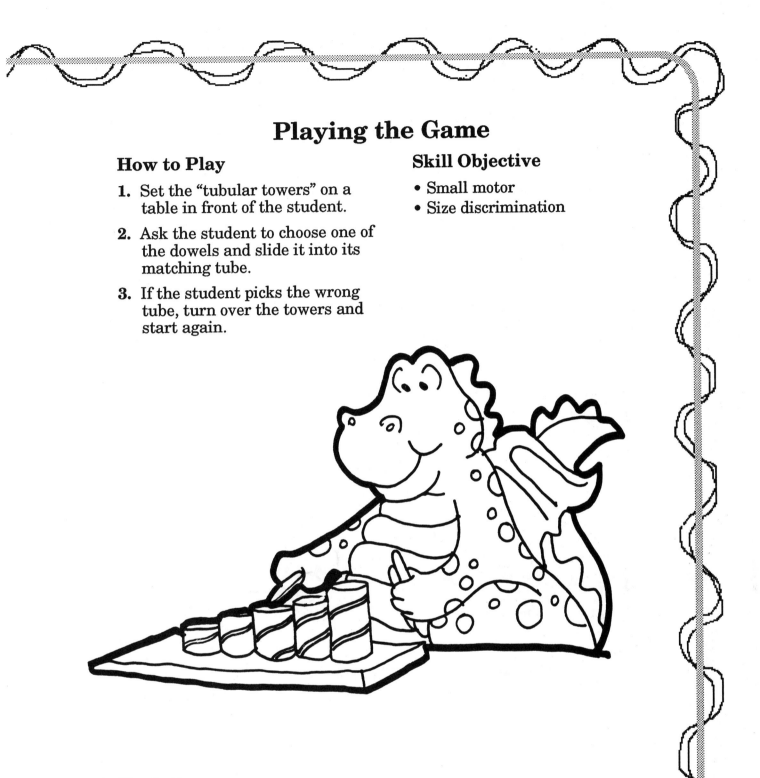

Variations

• For more advanced students: put the longest dowel in the shortest tube; put the shortest dowel in the longest tube, etc.

• Paint the dowels the same colors as their matching tubes. Ask the child to put the green dowel in the red tube, the yellow dowel in the blue tube, etc.

SHAPE CAPADE

Making the Game

Directions

1. Use heavy black marker to outline each object on individual 8 1/2" x 11" (21.5 cm x 28 cm) cardboard or tag board sheets.

2. Decorate a box with crayons or contact paper for storage.

3. Place the sheets and objects in the decorated box.

Materials

- 5 - 8 1/2" x 11" (21.5 cm x 28 cm) cardboard or tag board sheets

- 1 each: crayon, large paper clip, pencil, chalk-board eraser, small scotch tape dispenser

- Black marker pen

- Box to hold sheets and objects for storage

Playing the Game

How to Play

1. Place the "shape capade" sheets and objects on the table in front of the children.

2. Ask the children to place the object on the correct sheet.

Skill Objective

- Critical thinking
- Object recognition
- Hand-eye coordination

Variations

- Use objects that need to be manipulated in some way to fit the shape, such as scissors or plyers that are laying open on the page.

- Use objects that have two or three parts, such as a pen and cap that need to be matched to the outlines on the sheet exactly.

Making the Game

Directions

1. Cut the flaps off of the envelopes.
2. Cut index cards to fit inside the envelopes.
3. Write a 4-number sequence in the area of each index card that will show through the envelope window.
4. Write a duplicate set of the 4-number sequences on the envelopes next to the windows.
5. Laminate the index cards to make them more durable.

Materials

- 10 window envelopes
- 10 index cards
- Marker pen

Playing the Game

How to Play

1. Set out the envelopes and index cards on the table in front of the student.

2. Ask the student to look at the number sequence on one of the envelopes.

3. Instruct the student to pick out the index card with the matching 4-number sequence.

4. Slide in the card and watch it match up through the window.

Skill Objective

- Small motor
- Number recognition
- Visual discrimination

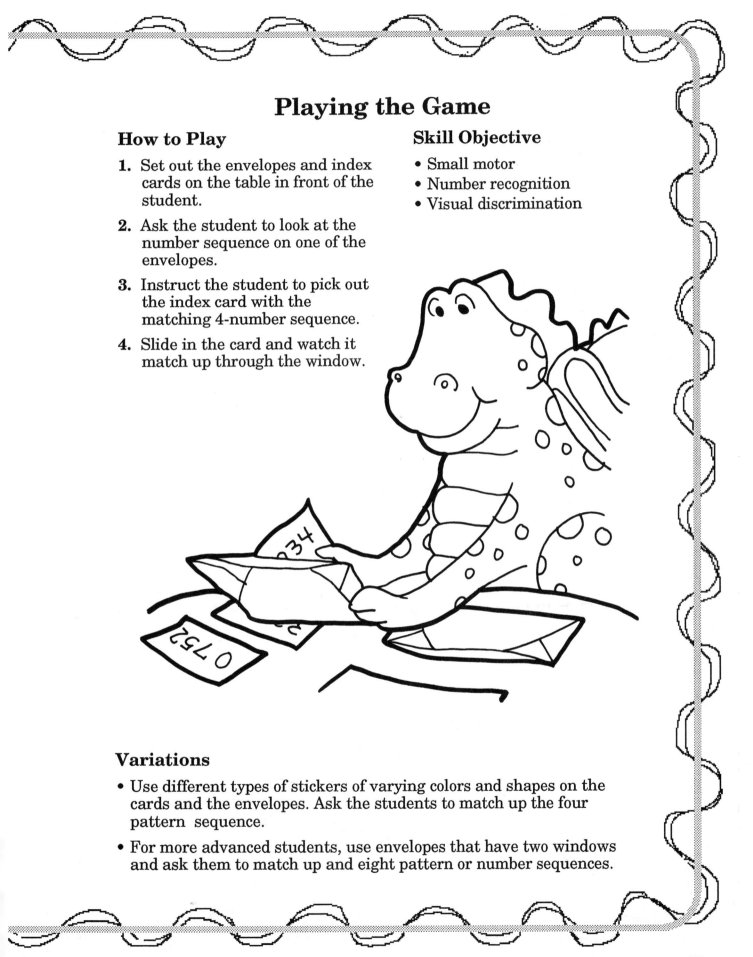

Variations

- Use different types of stickers of varying colors and shapes on the cards and the envelopes. Ask the students to match up the four pattern sequence.

- For more advanced students, use envelopes that have two windows and ask them to match up and eight pattern or number sequences.

CLOTHESPIN CLAMPERS

Making the Game

Directions

1. Divide each paint stirrer into nine sections by drawing a separating line with the marker.

2. In random order, write the letters of the alphabet in each space, upper and lower case. The third paint stirrer will only have eight letters. Draw a star in the last section.

3. Paint or mark a different letter on each clothespin, writing both upper and lower case letters. Draw a star on the last clothespin.

Materials

- 3 paint stirrers
- 27 wooden clothespins
- Marker pens or paint

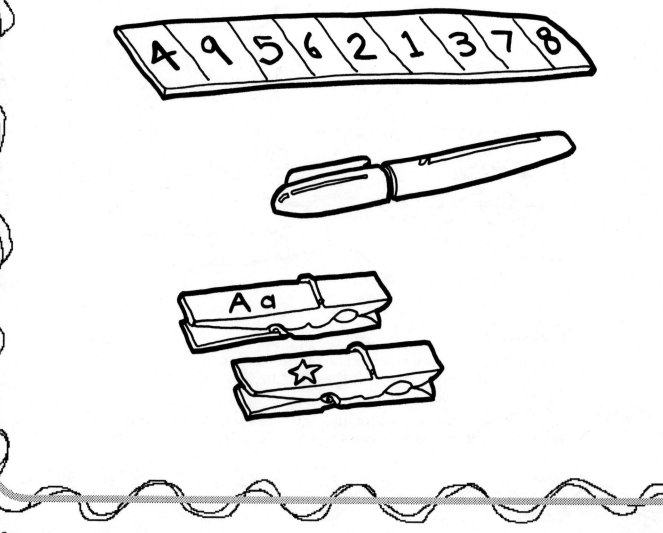

Playing the Game

How to Play

1. Place the paint stirrers and clothespins face up on the table.

2. Call out different letters and ask the student to clip the correct clothespin to the matching space on the paint stirrer.

3. If all the the letters are matched correctly, call out the star and clip it to the stirrer for a job well done!

Skill Objective

- Alphabet recognition
- Listening/Transfer
- Small motor

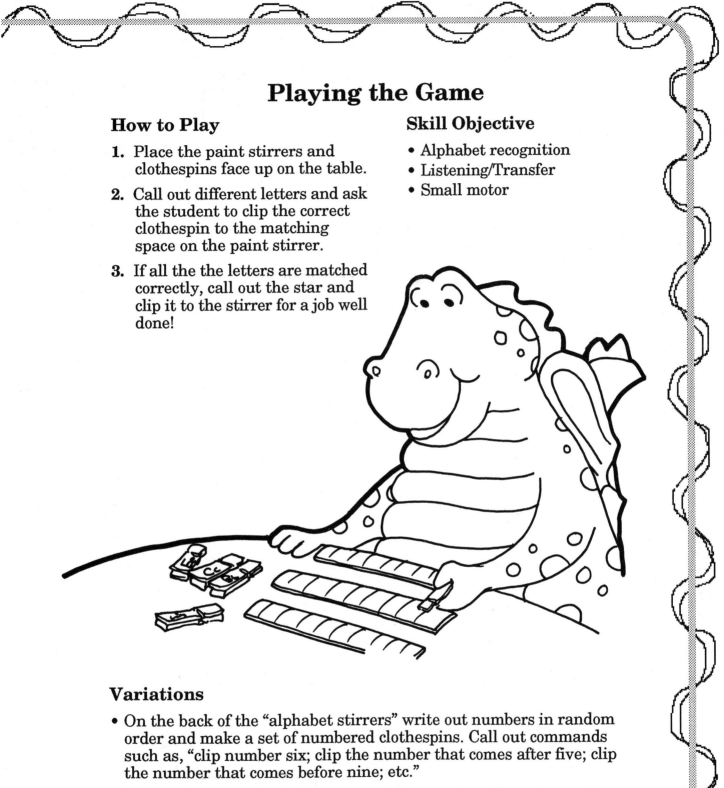

Variations

- On the back of the "alphabet stirrers" write out numbers in random order and make a set of numbered clothespins. Call out commands such as, "clip number six; clip the number that comes after five; clip the number that comes before nine; etc."

- On another set of stirrers, draw one dot, two dots, three dots and so on in random order. Write the corresponding numbers on a set of clothespins. Ask the students to match a clothespin to the correct number of dots on the paint stirrer.

Sock Hop Hamper

Making the Game

Directions

1. Ask each student to bring a clean pair of socks from home.

Materials

- 1 laundry basket
- 1 pair of socks for each student

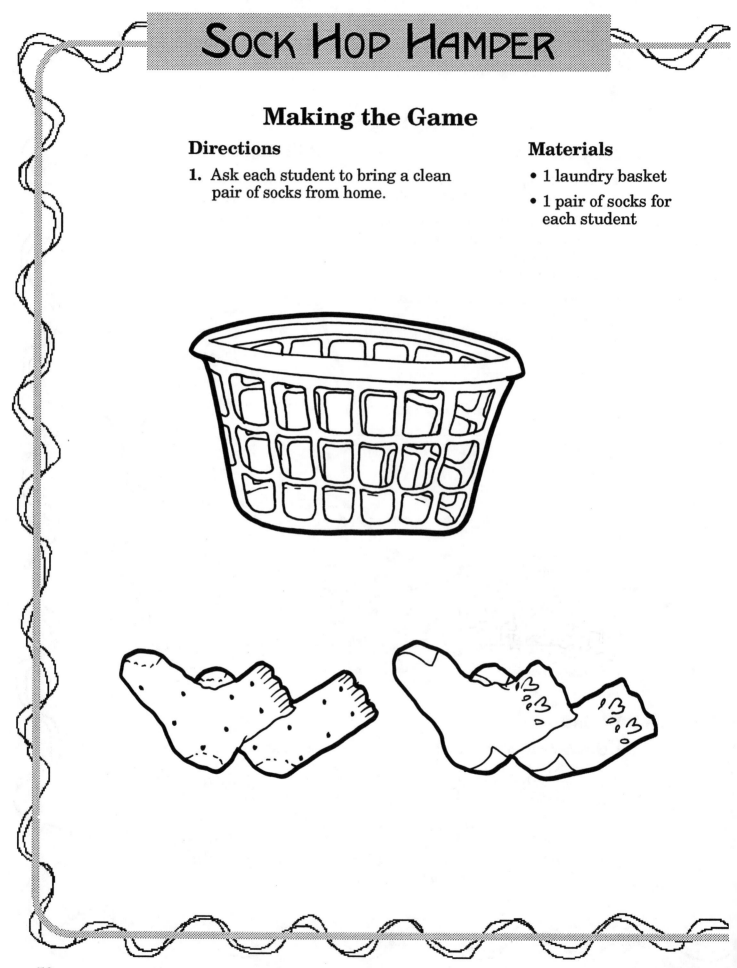

Playing the Game

How to Play

1. Ask the students to sit in a circle around the laundry basket.

2. Instruct them to take off their shoes and socks and put on one of the clean socks they brought for the game.

3. Place the matching socks in the hamper.

4. Have the students dig through the hamper one, two, or three at a time and find their matching sock. They should return to their place in the circle and put it on.

5. When all the socks are matched up have a sock hop by dancing around the room!

Skill Objective

- Visual discrimination
- Listening/Transfer
- Large & small motor

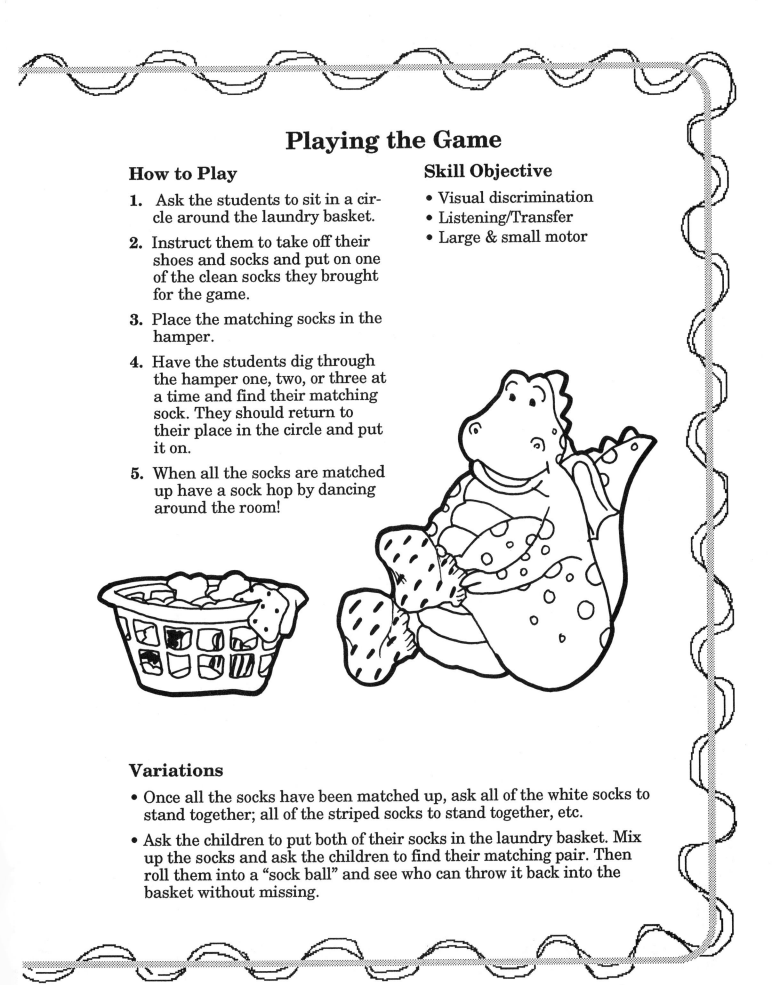

Variations

- Once all the socks have been matched up, ask all of the white socks to stand together; all of the striped socks to stand together, etc.

- Ask the children to put both of their socks in the laundry basket. Mix up the socks and ask the children to find their matching pair. Then roll them into a "sock ball" and see who can throw it back into the basket without missing.

DAIRY DELIGHT

Making the Game

Directions

1. Thoroughly wash out the empty milk cartons.

2. Fill two cartons completely with sand, two of the cartons 3/4 full, two - 1/2 full, two - 1/4 full, and two cartons leave empty.

3. Seal the tops of the cartons with masking or plastic tape.

Materials

- 10 - 1 quart (1 liter) milk cartons
- Sand
- Masking tape or colored plastic tape

Playing the Game

How to Play

1. Ask students to line up one set of cartons on the table from heaviest to lightest.

2. Then ask students to find each carton's match from the second group of cartons.

Skill Objective

• Weight discrimination
• Critical thinking

Variations

• Have the students work in pairs. Line up the cartons on the table. The first students picks up two cartons and asks which one is lighter. The second student feels the weight of the cartons and picks the lightest one or says they are the same.

GO TOGETHERS

Making the Game

Directions

1. Decorate the storage box with paint, crayons, or contact paper.

2. Assemble all the materials. If any are unavailable, substitute with associated pairs of your choosing.

3. Store all the materials in the decorated box.

Materials

- 1 box to hold the following objects:
- Plastic cup and saucer
- Shoe and sock
- Mitt and softball
- Comb and brush
- Pot and pot holder
- Fork and spoon
- Paint box and paint brush
- Soap and washcloth
- Paint, crayons or contact paper

Playing the Game

How to Play

1. Have children sit in a small group around a table or on the floor.

2. Place one part of each "go-together" set in the box. Place the other half of each "go-together" set on the table or floor.

3. Hold up an item from the box for the children to see.

4. Ask a child to pick its "go-together" from the middle of the floor or table.

5. Ask the group if they agree with the choice.

Skill Objective

- Association
- Critical thinking

Variations

- Instead of real objects, cut pictures from magazines and glue them to index cards to make a deck of "go-together" cards.

- Make a set of "go-together" cards that are made up of mother animals and their babies.

- If possible have the child demonstrate how the two objects work together.

CRAFTY COUNTERS

Making the Game

Directions

1. Wrap contact paper around each tube leaving the ends open.

2. Place the toilet paper rolls on the tagboard in one line so one of their open ends is facing up.

3. Glue each roll to the tagboard in this position with the sides of the rolls touching.

4. Using a thick black marker, write the numbers 1 through 10 on the rolls progressively from left to right.

Materials

- 10 toilet paper rolls
- 55 popsicle or craft sticks
- 8" x 22" (20 cm x 56 cm) tag board
- Contact paper
- Glue
- Thick black marker

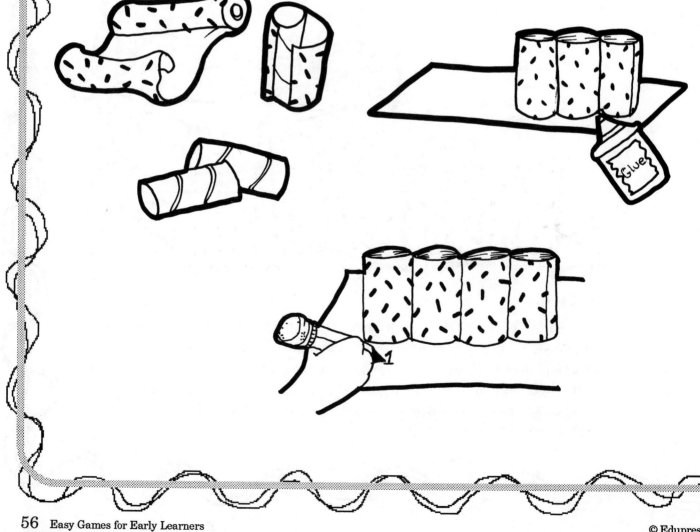

Playing the Game

How to Play

1. Place the "crafty counter" along with the 55 craft sticks in front of the student on a table.

2. Ask the student to put one craft stick in the "1" slot, two craft sticks in the "2" slot, etc.

3. Once the child has mastered this skill, call out various instructions such as find the number between seven and nine and put that many craft sticks in the slot.

Skill Objective

- Counting
- Left to right tracking

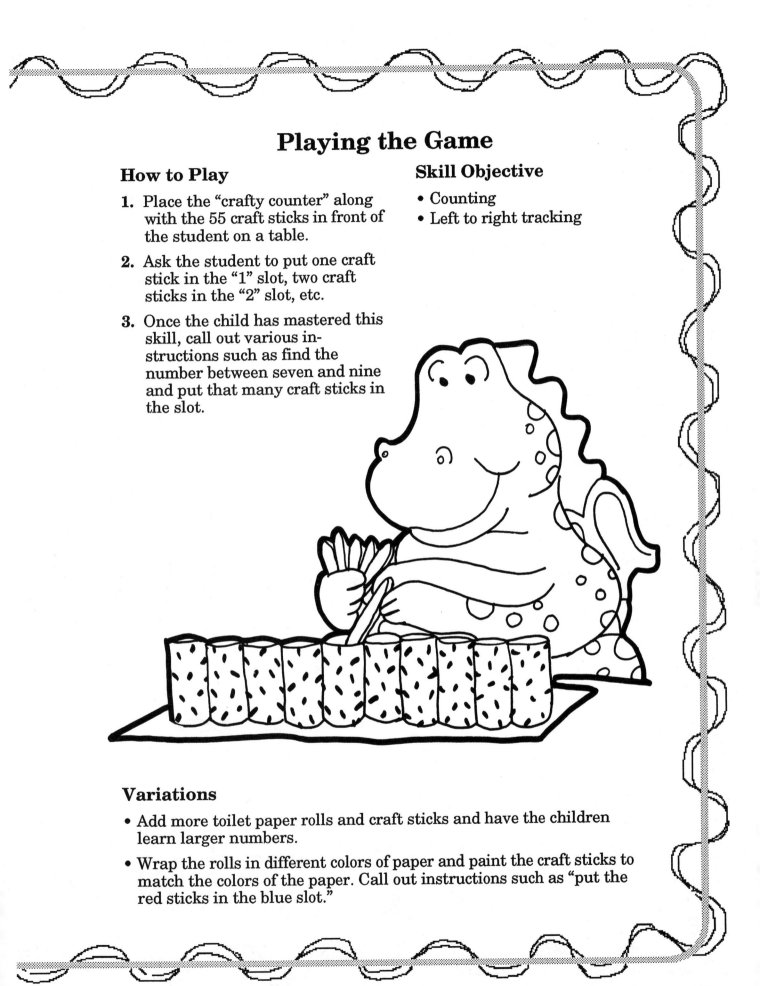

Variations

- Add more toilet paper rolls and craft sticks and have the children learn larger numbers.

- Wrap the rolls in different colors of paper and paint the craft sticks to match the colors of the paper. Call out instructions such as "put the red sticks in the blue slot."

Dinosaur Bones

Making the Game

Directions

1. Stuff one of the sports socks with fiberfill.

2. Put the second sock over the first to cover the open end.

3. Place rubber bands about 3" (7 cm) from each end to create a bone shape.

4. Repeat above instructions to create a total of five bones.

Materials

- 10 white sport socks (2 for each bone)
- Fiberfill
- 10 rubber bands (2 for each bone)

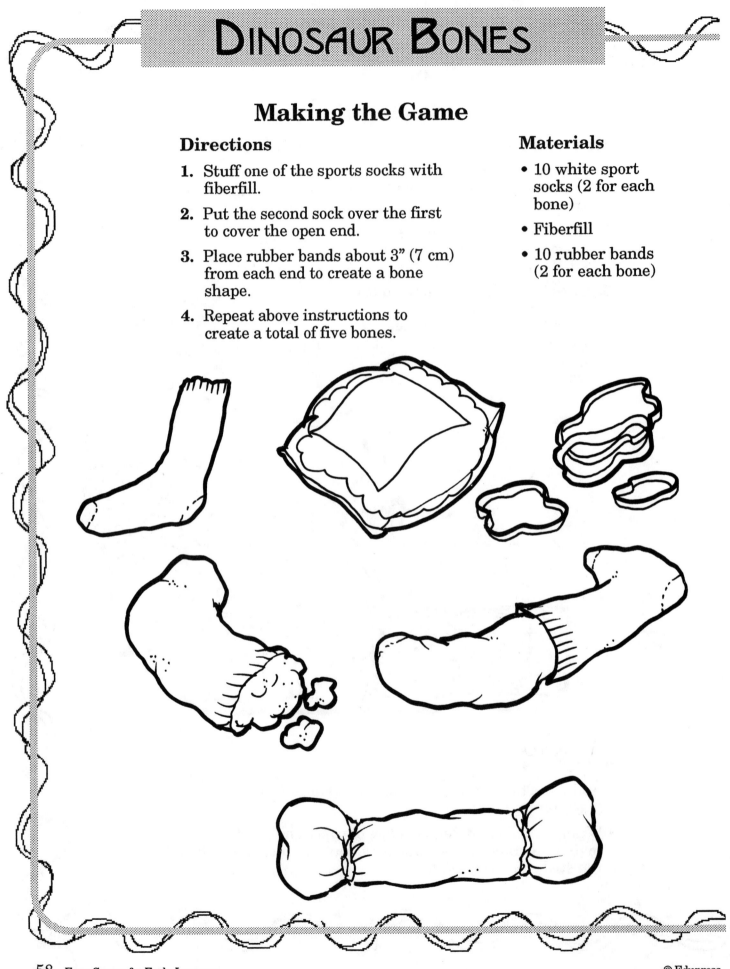

Playing the Game

How to Play

1. Select a student to hide the five bones in the classroom while the other children are watching.

2. Have all of the children make one trip around the classroom acting like dinosaurs.

3. Then choose one dinosaur to remember where all of the bones were hidden and bring them to the center of the room.

4. Hide the bones again.

Skill Objective

- Large motor
- Observation development
- Memory development

Variations

- Divide the children into small groups, and name them after dinosaurs. Ask the stegosaurus group to hide bones for the triceratops to find.

- Ask all of the dinosaurs to hide their eyes, while the bones are hidden. Have them hunt for the hidden bones. Any dinosaur that finds a bone may crawl around the room and make dinosaur sounds!

PEEKING PIRATES

Making the Game

Directions

1. Ask each student to decorate their telescope with paint, crayons or pieces of torn colored paper.

2. If decorating with torn paper, glue in place.

Materials

- Paper towel tube for each participating pirate
- Paint, crayons or colored paper
- Glue

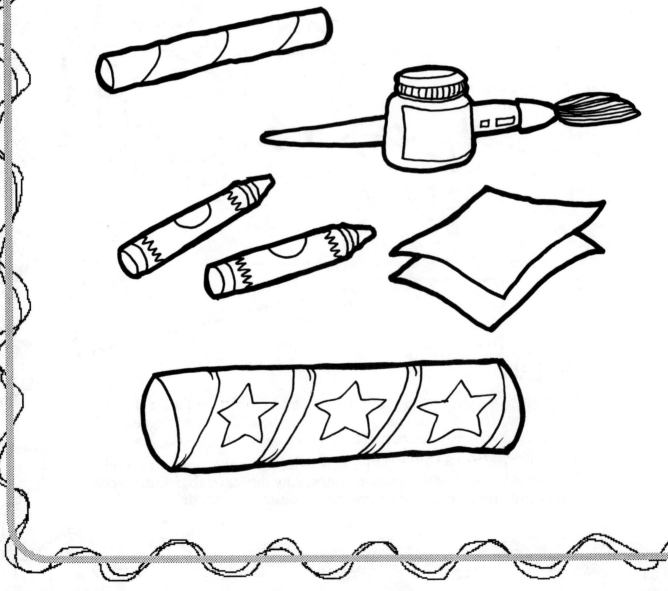

© Edupress

Playing the Game

How to Play

1. Give each "peeking pirate" a telescope.

2. Ask students to "peek" through their telescopes, scanning everywhere in the classroom.

3. Call out "freeze" and tell students to fix their gaze upon one object.

4. Call out three different shapes and colors such as, "who's peeking at a blue object? Who's peeking at a round object?" Ask the students to raise their hands if the object in sight has these characteristics.

5. Begin the game again, asking the children to scan the room for a different object.

Skill Objective

- Shape recognition
- Color recognition
- Listening/Transfer

Variations

- Add a second feature to each description, such as, "Who's peeking at something red and square."

- When "freeze" is called out, ask the children to, one by one, name their object and say what color it is.

- Call out a letter of the alphabet and ask the children to find an object that begins with that letter sound.

NUMBER NOODLES

Making the Game

Directions

1. Holding the tagboard vertically, write the numbers 1 through 10 down the left side of the tag board, about two inches from the edge of the sheet.

2. Write the numbers 1 through 10 in random order along the right side, about two inches in from the edge.

3. Punch a hole to the right of each number on the tagboard.

4. Reinforce the holes with the paper reinforcements.

5. Thread one shoe lace through each hole on the left side, tying a knot on the back and on the front so that it cannot be pulled through.

Materials

- 12" x 18" (30 cm x 45 cm) tagboard
- 10 shoe laces
- Hole punch
- Paper hole reinforcements
- Scissors
- Heavy marker

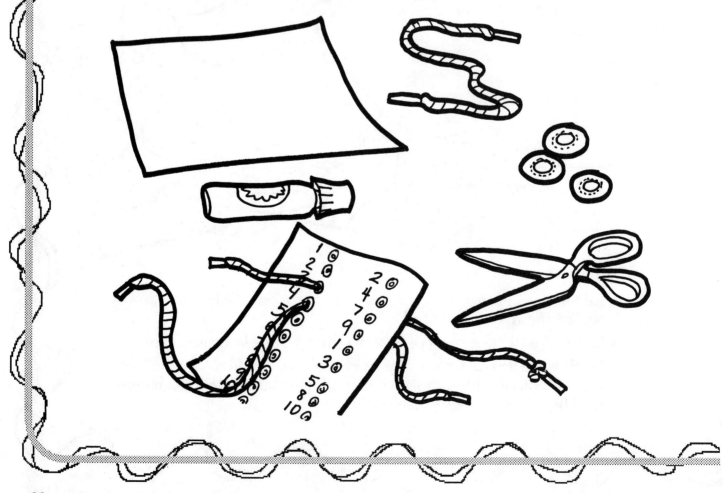

Playing the Game

How to Play

1. Place the "number noodles" board in front of the student on the table.

2. Ask the student to look at the first number on the left and then find its matching number on the right.

3. Thread the shoe lace to connect the matching numbers.

4. Working down the left hand side, continue matching the numbers.

Skill Objective

- Number recognition
- Number sequencing

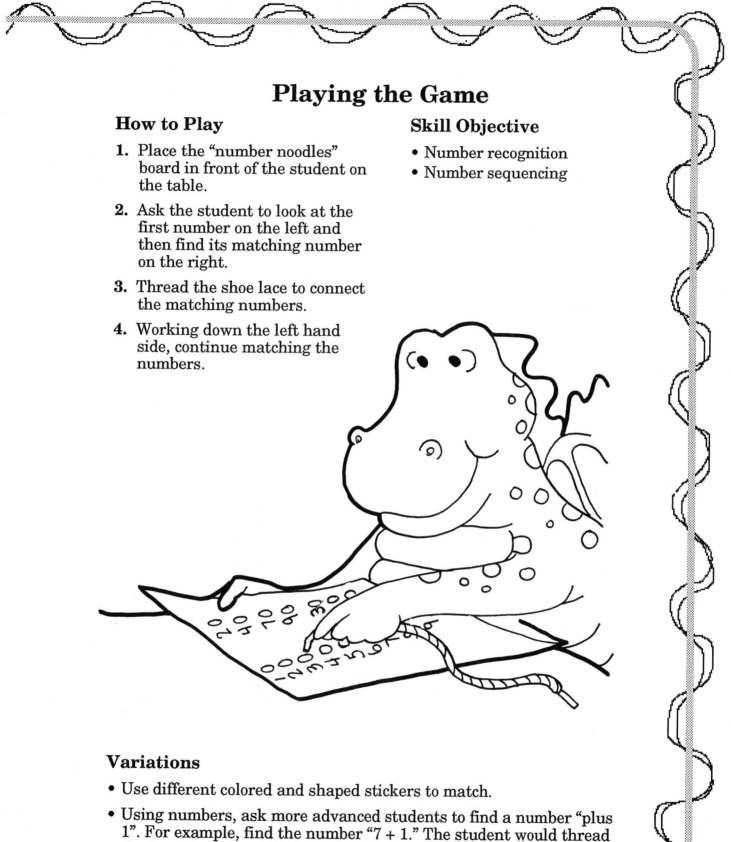

Variations

- Use different colored and shaped stickers to match.

- Using numbers, ask more advanced students to find a number "plus 1". For example, find the number "7 + 1." The student would thread the lace through number eight.

More Exciting Titles from **Edupress**

139 Super Arts & Crafts
Over 700 art activities

153 Make It Today
Easy-to-make equipment

154 Theme Day Play
20 Fun-filled days

152 Easy Games
Easy-to-make games

130 Fall Projects
Multicurricular learning

144 Literature Patterns
Interact with literature

145 Alphabet Patterns
Hands-on activities

146 Scissor Skill Patterns
Cut-and-learn fun

131 Winter Projects
Loads of winter activities

123 Holiday Patterns
A host of holiday fun

125 Puppet Patterns
Multicurricular activities

124 Poem Patterns
Link poems & learning

135 Center Games
Ten easy game centers

136 Outdoor Games
Group and skill games

134 Holiday Games
Games for every holiday

111 Lend An Ear
Build listening skills